ALIGNMENT, PROCESS, RELATIONSHIPS

STEVE KING

ALIGNMENT, PROCESS, RELATIONSHIPS
A Simple Guide to Team Management

ALIGNMENT, PROCESS, RELATIONSHIPS
A SIMPLE GUIDE TO TEAM MANAGEMENT

iUniverse books may be ordered through booksellers or by contacting:

iUniverse
1663 Liberty Drive
Bloomington, IN 47403
www.iuniverse.com
1-800-Authors (1-800-288-4677)

ISBN: 978-1-5320-6823-2 (sc)
ISBN: 978-1-5320-6824-9 (e)

Library of Congress Control Number: 2019901528

Print information available on the last page.

iUniverse rev. date: 02/15/2019

Dedication

To Betsy, Lisa, and Artell, for your enduring partnership, and to Michelle, for your enduring love and encouragement

Contents

Introduction

1

I spend a good deal of time with frontline managers and supervisors. I make time to be with them because I find it a grounding experience. You want to know what's going on in an organization? They know. They can tell you the real story about millennials, the impact of continuous improvement efforts, and whether corporate policies work as intended. They see productivity issues firsthad. They can make or break most change efforts.

I wrote my first two books—*Brag, Worry, Wonder, Bet* and *Six Conversations*—with them in mind. I wanted to provide managers with simple tools and techniques to better manage their staffs.

So when they asked for something more, I was all ears. The questions on their minds had to do with their teams. How can they better manage their teams? How can they get the most out of their teams? Can they apply the same techniques they use with individual members of the team to the team as a whole?

Typically, I punted on these questions. I tried wedging into team situations the tools that worked in one-on-one situations. I suggested they read the *Five Dysfunctions of a Team* by Patrick Lencioni and *The Wisdom of Teams* by Jon Katzenbach and Douglas Smith. I recommend those reads to anyone interested in team development. They are classics and deserve a spot on any manager's bookshelf. However, I felt like I was coming up short on providing the same simple, practical advice I'd offered in my earlier work.

It turns out that that simple, practical advice was hidden in plain sight in my consulting practice.

I am constantly being asked to work with teams. The requests often sound like one of the following:

- The team just seems to be on different pages from one another. We're running in different directions. Can you help?
- The team is stepping over one another as we rush to get things done. Are there ways for us to collaborate better?
- The team has lost faith in one another. Trust is ebbing, and it's affecting our work. Can we get back the trust?

While these three questions are posed as distinctly different questions, they are seriously intertwined. Trust breaks down when people are on different pages. A lack of role clarity—even when the goals are crystal clear—can lead to questions about team members' competencies. Personal agendas drive competing goals that are hidden from other team members.

To sort out this convergence of team dynamics, I began using a three-part framework to assess and address team issues. I started calling the framework "alignment, process, and relationships," and for some reason, I drew it on a flip chart or whiteboard as a triangle with a word at each point:

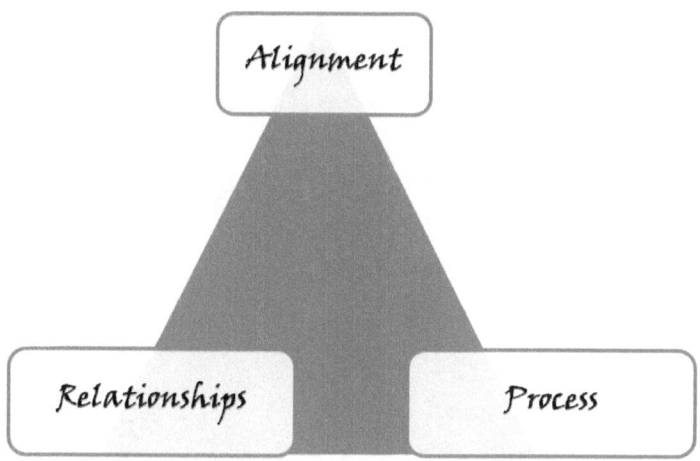

Managers and their teams quickly latched on to this framework and found success using it to address team issues and concerns. This book offers details behind this framework and advice and ways to use it successfully. As we examine the details, we'll also address two related topics that inevitably show up: team culture and managing difficult individual behavior. As we venture into these topics, we won't stray too far from the three anchoring notions of alignment, process, and relationships.

A small sidebar before we get started: This book has been written with frontline, intact work teams in mind. A good deal of what we will cover here applies nicely to other kinds of teams, including project teams, virtual teams, executive leadership teams, middle-management teams, and self-directed teams. However, there are subtle differences. If you find yourself running one of these other teams and are applying the concepts from this book, stay alert and be prepared to improvise a bit.

Alignment, Process, Relationships: The Basics

2

What I love about a bell-shaped curve is that it is a reminder that most of us, most of the time, have similar experiences. Most of the time, we live on the fat part of a bell-shaped curve. Those experiences on either end of the curve are the exceptional, more unusual moments.

Considering what makes a team successful is a bell-shaped exercise. Special team circumstances can suggest sophisticated analysis and solutions, but success is usually a function of a few factors that a manager can understand and master. In this book, we will explore three of those factors.

> To put it plainly, teams need to be aligned, they need good process, and they need good relationships.

To put it plainly, teams need to be aligned, they need good process, and they need good relationships. If you meet these three conditions, there is a very good chance a team can be successful.

Here is a snapshot of what I mean by team alignment, process, and relationships. I'll put some meat on these bones later.

Alignment is about team goals:

- Are your team goals explicit and clear?
- Are the metrics for these goals explicit and clear?

- Does your team have key behavioral goals the whole team understands and conforms to?
- Can you link those behavioral goals to more business-oriented goals?
- Do your team goals align with your department and organizational goals?
- Do you incent your team to achieve the stated goals?

Process is about team execution:

- Are members of your team clear about their roles and responsibilities? Are the "decision rights" of your team members clear to each of them?
- Is there a clear purpose for your team meetings?
- Is there an opportunity for your team to assess its performance in a team setting? Does this opportunity to assess lead to improvements in team alignment, process, and relationships?
- Are your team's work processes understood and aligned with larger organizational goals?

Relationships are about team dynamics:

- Does your team trust each other professionally and personally?
- Are legitimate disagreements on your team handled effectively?
- Does each member of your team have a reasonable amount of emotional intelligence?
- Are the group dynamics of the team healthy and productive?

If you happen to answer yes to every one of those questions, congratulations. You probably don't need to read any further.

For those of you reading on, some of these questions are not easily addressed by a manager. How does a manager ensure all team members trust one another? It's not easy. I'll address each of these questions in the coming chapters, but first, here's an observation about the relationship between these three conditions of team success.

Consider a pit crew at the Indy 500 on any Memorial Day weekend. Each member of the crew has his or her own goals, like changing a tire within a certain amount of time, but the whole crew has the collective goal of getting their driver safely back on the track as quickly as possible. They are aligned. Each pit crew member has his or her own assigned responsibility and a specified process to execute that responsibility. They have the right tools to get the job done. They have a process. The crew needs a high level of trust in one another to get their jobs done and be willing to ask for help when it is needed—in this case partly because it is a dangerous activity. They need relationships.

The same is true in less dangerous workplaces. Consider a fast-food restaurant. Each member of the crew has their own goals, but the whole crew has the collective goal of getting hot food to the customer quickly. Each crew member has their own assigned responsibility and a specified process to execute that responsibility. They need to be following a well-planned process and have the right tools. The crew needs to trust one another to get their jobs done and be willing to ask for help when it is needed.

The synchronicity of alignment, process, and relationships is what gets the job done well. Good alignment with poor process and poor relations just does not cut it. You need all three. The job of the manager is to create that synchronicity.

What is interesting about this framework is that there is a casual pecking order to the three conditions. It is hard to build good process without goals, and relationships can be tenuous if good process is not informing the relationship. So, a general rule of thumb when a manager is trying to build a better team is first tend to alignment, then tend to process, and then tend to relationships.

I know this flies in the face of conventional thinking that trust is always the first order of team business. Trust is essential, but misalignment and poor process can breed mistrust and weaken relationships. If a manager is prioritizing work with the team, they might as well tend to the prerequisite conditions before beginning a full-frontal assault on relationship issues.

Before we get into some of the nitty-gritty of the framework, let's take a moment to acknowledge that not all teams are created equal.

Wrestling Teams and
Football Teams

3

Consider the difference between a high school wrestling team and a high school football team. Wrestling teams are made up of a handful of individuals who go out to the mat, wrestle opponents from other schools, and win or lose individual points for their team. The team score is simply the sum of the individual scores. A football team, on the other hand, is a choreographed team activity where scoring requires a collective effort—and the team score is the result of that collective effort.

Is a wrestling team really a team? Yes, I think so. The team score matters. Members of the team support one another with encouragement, tips, and feedback. The coach must strategize and determine which wrestlers will wrestle which opponents. However, it is a different kind of team than a football team, which is a more collaborative experience.

There are wrestling teams and football teams in business settings as well. In some businesses, work can only get done when the staff's efforts are deeply coordinated. Consider rush hour in a family restaurant. The whole staff—waiters, cooks, busboys, dishwashers, and hosts—is moving in sync to get meals served to waves of customers. When it is done well, it is a thing of beauty. It is like a football team.

There are wrestling teams and football teams in business settings as well.

Consider a call center with twenty service representatives. Most of the calls are one-and-done interactions. These individual efforts are like a wrestling team. Of course, in the call center environment, there is teamwork. Some calls need to be transferred to other team members. The IT folks are available to troubleshoot systems issues, but the basic routine is a solo effort for those on the phones.

This distinction about teams is important because the application of alignment, process, and relationships is a little different in each case. Interestingly, teams that resemble football teams are often easier to manage since the team dynamic is so apparent and clear. A waiter is very aware that his tip is somewhat contingent on the performance of those in the kitchen, and he will probably make efforts to coordinate with the kitchen. That is not the case with a call center representative who can be successful despite the other reps. Motivating that call center service rep to care about the team is trickier.

Imagine two sales managers. One manager has a team of salespeople with their own sales quotes, and they can pursue sales as they wish. The other manager has a team with a team sales goal in addition to individual sales quotas, and they are expected to coordinate their sales efforts. How will these two sales managers set goals, establish compensation, and give feedback on sales performance?

In the case of the first sales manager, sales goals, compensation, and feedback are probably handled one salesperson at a time. The second sales manager will meet individually with the sales force, but they will also need to work with the team on collective goals, create a compensation structure that incents the group to work together, and provide feedback to the team as a group.

Different kinds of teams have different managerial tactics.

Team Goals: "What's Expected of Us?"

4

I'll start with stating the obvious. Team goals are those goals the team is held responsible for. They will be assessed as a team, and they will be rewarded as a team when the goals are met. A team without team goals is just a group occupying a workspace. For some businesses, that may be fine, but for most, groups simply occupying a workspace represents lost productivity.

> Team goals originate from two places: the requirements of the team's customers and the cascading goals from higher up in the organization.

Team goals originate from two places: the requirements of the team's customers and the cascading goals from higher up in the organization. The first order of business for a team leader is talking with customers about what they need from the team and making sure they understand what their boss and their boss's boss need from the team. Once that data is collected, I encourage managers to bring the team together, review the data, and knock out a draft of team goals over a few team meetings.

I know I just made it sound so easy—and sometimes it is. If the team's customers are known—and the needs and goals of senior management are clear and explicit—a draft of team goals can come together quickly.

A recruiting team's customers (hiring managers) might say they want their jobs filled within thirty days, and senior management might say they want the cost of recruiting to stay below a number. A time-to-fill goal of thirty days and a cost per hire of $500 could reasonably become the recruiting team's goals.

However, plenty of things can get in the way of setting team goals so easily. For example, visiting with customers and senior management is not a one-and-done exercise. These ongoing, ever-changing relationships can make team goals a moving set of targets. Customers and senior management can change their minds. A team manager needs to establish an ongoing dialogue with these groups to make sure the team's goals stay aligned with customer needs and senior management's expectations.

For some team managers, things can be even more complicated. Customers or higher-ups may be unclear about what they want. In highly matrixed organizations, the team manager may report to more than one person and have multiple bosses who are not on the same page.

Managers facing these challenges need to be diligent in seeking clarity. Ask for it. Argue that clarity will bring better results and greater productivity, but if that clarity does not come, the manager should consider creating de facto or temporary goals to serve as placeholders until clarity arrives. Create these with the team's input and with the best information available. If those placeholders are created, the manager needs to make the de facto goals transparent. Tell everyone—customers, senior management, and suppliers—what those goals are so everyone is on the same page, even if it is a temporary page. The presence of temporary goals can sometimes elevate conversations with customers and senior leaders, which allows their real goals to emerge. In those cases, the team manager's persistence can help everyone.

Like goals for individual members of a team, team goals should be SMART: *specific, measurable, attainable, relevant,* and *timely.* This way, assessment of success can be pinpointed with some accuracy. For the recruiting team, a team goal might read something like this: "The recruiting team will, in this fiscal year, fill all open positions for Division X within thirty days at an average cost of no more than $500 per hire."

Metrics, Team Behaviors, and Incentives

5

Team goals are no different than goals for individuals. They are better when there are clear metrics. In the previous recruiting example, the metrics were clear—time to fill was thirty days, average cost per hire was $500, 100 percent of the open positions were in the mix, and the time-related metric was one fiscal year.

I have spoken to many team managers who are hesitant to attach clear metrics to team goals. The reasons are varied. Some have no expectations from customers or senior management and think, *Why bother?* They have a point. Some fear the accountability that clear metrics suggest. My experience is these managers might dodge being held accountable for a while, but eventually, it will catch up to them since, in the absence of explicit metrics, others assign their own imagined metrics to the expected team performance and judge accordingly. Some team managers simply don't know how.

How does a team manager select the right metrics? It partly comes from conversations about expectation with customers and senior management. Ask them their opinions. It partly comes from conversations with the team about reasonable metrics. They know the work better than anyone else, and their insights should inform any final decisions. Of course, the experience of the managers should be factored in. These perspectives—informed with historical data from past performances—should be the key inputs for selecting the right team goals.

Team goals that are directed at business results or processes can usually have a metric assigned to them. Business result goals have to do with things like revenue and expense targets, productivity targets, customer satisfaction targets, or even employee retention targets. Business process goals have to do with things like machine downtime, call center call drop rates, or number of sales calls per month.

> There is another kind of team goal that does not lend itself easily to metrics: behavioral goals.

There is another kind of team goal that does not lend itself easily to metrics: behavioral goals. The best teams I have observed have made explicit certain behavior norms expected of everyone on the team. Everyone on the team knows these are the expected behaviors and when someone does not behave accordingly, they are likely to be called out on it. In fact, that is probably the best definition of an "institutionalized" behavior norm or goal—when someone is called out for misbehaving.

Here are three examples of team behavior goals:

- If someone is overwhelmed with the work on his plate, he asks someone else on the team for help.
- If someone is asked to do something by a customer, she drops what she is doing and helps the customer.
- If someone has a better way of doing something, make sure this better idea is shared with someone with the authority to make a change happen.

These behavior norms or goals don't—and shouldn't—show up out of thin air. They should reflect one or more of the team's business goals. The first example is the kind of behavioral goal that is common on football-like teams. For those teams, work is so interdependent that one bottleneck affects them all. Hence, asking for help is good for the team. The second example is the kind of behavior goal derived from a strategic intention of a team to provide exceptional customer service. The third example is the kind of goal derived from a team intention to constantly drive for improvements in quality.

How are team behavior goals determined? Look carefully at the team's business goals, and through a series of conversations with the team, determine a few behaviors that are essential to those goals. Three or four will do. If there are too many, they will get lost in the shuffle of daily routines. Hold one another accountable for the behavioral goals. No metrics are needed—just accountability.

Team incentives are rewards given to the whole team for meeting or exceeding team goals. If there are team goals, there should be team incentives. The incentives don't necessarily have to be equal. Some team members could receive something more or something different than others upon the achievement of team goals, but it is not a team incentive unless everyone on the team is rewarded somehow. Team bonuses, stock options, or performance shares? Sure.

Plenty of teams don't have direct monetary rewards available, but there are other rewards: time off, company swag, dinner out for the family, or a professional conference. Managers should provide the rewards for achieving team goals that will be meaningful to team members and consistent with the cultural norms of the business. For example, if the company is all about being family friendly, time off might be a better choice than a professional conference.

Roles, Responsibilities, and Decision Rights

On a wrestling team, the roles of the team members are pretty much the same. Everyone wrestles. A few teams in the workplace are built the same way. Everyone does the same thing.

However, most workplace teams are made up of roles with slightly or dramatically different responsibilities. In a fast-food restaurant, there is a person at the fryer, a person at the grill, and a person at the counter. It is the same team with the same team goal, but there are different roles and responsibilities. The manager's job is to make sure each member of the team knows their role and responsibilities and how those roles and responsibilities sync up with the work of other team members.

Early in my career, I was part of a team responsible for building process-improvement capabilities for four thousand bankers. The team goal would have been written like this: "Provide six days of process improvement training to all bank employees over a two-year period, including personalized coaching for implementation of process-improvement activities assigned at the end of the six days of training."

Karen was the team manager, and she set up the roles and responsibilities.

Steve – me - selected program content, designed the six days of training, taught the first few offerings, and coached other instructors.

Ronnis taught, developed the facilitator's guide, and recruited and managed internal and external instructors.

Russ managed the development and distribution of all training materials for all classes and managed the program-evaluation process.

Ginny set up coaching arrangements, recruited and managed internal and external coaches for the post-program improvement activities, and coached the coaches.

Judy registered all program and coaching participants.

Part of the reason our little team worked so well—we accomplished the team goal and were still getting along after two years—was because the roles and responsibilities were so clear. There were no job descriptions for what we were doing because that formality was not necessary. Karen simply explained the team goals and expectations—and off we went. For some teams, written descriptions might help. If your team needs that type of formality to set the roles and responsibilities, then make it happen.

There was another reason why our team succeeded. The decision rights were clear. Decision rights indicate who can make the final decision to proceed with a particular task, who must be consulted before that decision is made, and who must be informed. For my team, I had the decision rights for all program content and design. I had the final say. It was expected though, before I made any final content or design decisions, that I consult with Ronnis and Russ since their input from a facilitation and materials-development perspective could inform my final decisions. Ginny could be informed after the fact, and any relevant program content change could be incorporated into coaching schemes.

> Decision rights indicate who can make the final decision to proceed with a particular task, who must be consulted before that decision is made, and who must be informed.

Some of you might recognize my description of decision rights as a kind of RACI analysis. RACI stands for *responsible, accountable, consulted,* and *informed.* This kind of analysis sorts out, for any given task within a process, who is responsible and accountable for that task, who must be consulted before the task is executed, and who must be informed once the task is completed. If you don't know what a RACI analysis is, google it. Plenty of great RACI resources are available online.

Whether or not you engage in a formal RACI exercise, the bottom line about decision rights is clarifying the ownership of key decisions and insisting on collaboration with the right team members before key decisions are made. If you don't, you run the risk of process confusion (Who's on first?) and relationship issues (That's my job! That's not my job! I wasn't included!). If you do, team efficiency and effectiveness will increase, and confusion and wasted energy will decrease.

Process Management and
Team Management

7

With frontline managers, I often ask, "How many processes do you and your team own and are responsible for?" Interestingly, most managers are not sure.

This is troubling since—besides managing people—managing process is probably the most important task on a manager's plate. In fact, managing people and managing process are interlocking responsibilities. To manage any process well, a manager must know the process and effectively assign team members to execute each step in the process. Think of the latter as the assignment of team roles and responsibilities.

A manager should be able to outline each process as a process map: depict each step in the process, name who is responsible for each step, identify what inputs are needed to complete each step and what outputs are created by the step, and include a definition of the quality of those outputs. Mapping process with the team's input is recommended. If they do the work, they know the process. When the team sees the whole process and their individual responsibilities within that larger process, they can begin to see how individual efforts become a team effort.

Here is a simple bookkeeping process map to illustrate the notion:

The bookkeeping manager and the team outline the process. Then the team defines any important inputs (perhaps a systems requirement) and key outputs (perhaps acknowledgement by the group receiving the distribution). The manager assigns team members responsibility for each step. Quality standards are established (perhaps the payer must be informed within twenty-four hours) and completed. This is process and team management.

Oddly enough, not all work is process. Most jobs follow scripts of sorts—processes, procedures, protocols, and policies—and creating process maps for these is reasonably easy and recommended. Other jobs are unscripted and are performed more by following some guiding principles (keep a work area clean, pay attention to the details, keep the customer's needs in mind, etc.) than scripted processes. In these cases, the manager and the team need to name those principles and consider turning them into behavioral goals for the team.

> Oddly enough, not all work is process.

When the team outlines a process, two questions should be asked: How does this process contribute to achieving the team's goals? How does this process contribute to achieving the larger goals of the organization? There is a casual pecking order to alignment, process, and relationships. Process management should take its cues from alignment to team goals and organizational goals. Some teams become enamored with the process and lose sight of the purpose of the process—the team goals. You don't want that to happen.

Team Meetings and Assessing Team Performance

8

There are so many good resources about how to run a good team meeting that I am not going to get into the conventional dos and don'ts of meeting management. If your team meetings are suffering, find help and improve them.

> Team meetings play a big role in creating alignment and managing process.

Team meetings play a big role in creating alignment and managing process. I recommend using team meetings to get input into creating team business goals and team behavioral goals. I also recommend using team meetings to map out team processes and get input into processes-quality standards.

Team meetings can play an important role as forums for the assessment of team performance. In my two other books—*Brag, Worry, Wonder, Bet* and *Six Conversations*—I make the conventional case that feedback is essential to performance improvement and suggest a rather unconventional way to provide feedback. For readers who have not read those earlier editions, here is the feedback framework I recommend managers use in situations like performance reviews.

- When I brag about you, here is what I brag about ...
- When I worry about you, here is what I worry about ...
- When I wonder about you, here is what I wonder about ...
- If I were to bet on you, here is what I would bet on ...

What works for providing individuals feedback works for teams as well. I, and many others, adopted this framework in team meetings to allow the team to self-assess its performance. It works quite simply. Once a quarter, in a team meeting, each person on the team writes down their brags, worries, wonders, and bets about the team. We go around the table and share our perspectives.

The brags often turn into recognition moments or even mild celebrations. Worries become the stuff of team-improvement plans, reconsidered goals, future process-improvement efforts, and changes to behaviors that could improve relationships. Wonders often bring up questions about the future of the team's work and the future of organization's expectations for the team when change is afoot. Bets turn into risk assessments, and the team imagines the likelihood of success going forward.

Once the team gets in a rhythm of doing these quarterly assessments, good things happen. One person who used this approach to team assessment told me that the quarterly meetings established team process-improvement efforts that became the fodder for weekly team meetings. Perhaps the most important thing that happens is team performance improves over time when feedback surfaces and is acted upon.

Professional Trust, Personal Trust, and Emotional Intelligence

9

Trust is the backbone of any relationship—

> Trust is the backbone of any relationship—inside or outside of work.

inside or outside of work. Trust in a work setting is partly about competency. If the person working next to me is incompetent, I may not trust them to do what needs to be done. And if my work team is more like a football team, this becomes a team issue.

Of course, there are more fundamental trust issues than lack of competence. Some people lie at work. Some people steal at work. Some people cheat at work.

I am often asked to work with a team because the team has "trust problems." Before jumping directly into solving relationship issues like trust, I explore any alignment and process issues that are polluting team relations and creating distrust.

Some teams have relationship issues that are singularly rooted in trust issues. When that is apparent, I ask, "Is this a personal trust issue between team members—or is it a professional trust issue?"

Personal trust is sort of like integrity. If someone says they are going to do something, they can be counted on to do it. If you tell someone something in confidence, it remains confidential—and the person does not go blabbing it to everyone else the first chance they get. Over the years, I have had a few people like that on my teams. It tends to erode team relationships quickly.

Professional trust is more about how well we do our jobs and how competent we are. When you are working with someone who is not very good at their job, team handoffs can be awkward. If a manager has a salesperson who is not very good, the rest of the team will hesitate to transfer clients to them—and the manager may hesitate to assign new territories. That kind of trust issue can slowly erode team relationships.

Whether trust erodes quickly or slowly, its impact on team performance is clearly negative. Goals become harder to achieve. Processes sub-optimize. Alignment, process, and relationships are all interconnected.

What should a manager do to ensure personal trust exists on their teams? First, seek to hire people who clearly exhibit *emotional intelligence*. These people recognize and effectively manage their own emotions, and they are good at recognizing and effectively relating to the emotions of others. The breakthrough insight from research on emotional intelligence is that those with it perform better. It is one of the best indicators that personal trust will be brought into the team from the get-go. So, managers should use every opportunity to recruit for it.

Managers should be vigilant about such behaviors on the team and seek to remedy them immediately. Swift and direct action when it comes to personal trust issues is the best course of action. Perhaps let a little thing or one out-of-character moment slide; otherwise, address this kind of trust issue quickly and decisively. This is not something that should be allowed to continue and fester. A later chapter explores how to address those kinds of trust issues.

Managers almost universally agree that dealing with professional trust issues is easier than dealing with personal trust issues, but not every competency issue is easily solved. It just does not carry the same emotional baggage as personal trust issues.

Since professional trust issues stem from a lack of competence, employee development is the first corrective action. In *Six Conversations,* I devoted a few chapters to an employee question: "What and how should I develop?" This is relevant when dealing with professional trust issues on a team—whether it is one team member or many.

To address how he or she might develop, the manager, with the help of an employee, should clearly name the skill or knowledge that is lacking. Second, the manager and employee should follow the 70/20/10 rule (learn by doing: 70 percent, learn from feedback: 20 percent, and learn in virtual or real classrooms: 10 percent) and create a plan to build those skills. For example, if a team member lacks project management skills, give them an opportunity to lead a small project (70), give them an experienced project manager to provide feedback and guidance on the employee's execution of the project (20), and have the employee take a good project-management program to learn the basics of the skill (10). Most of the time, this approach will remedy the professional trust issues. However, if it does not, the manager should consider reassignment of the weak performer to a new role in the organization where their skills are better suited for success.

Trust is so important to team dynamics and team performance, and if efforts to deal with it fail, the final option is dismissal. This is not an option most managers relish, but it is a necessary one. The drama created by a lack of trust on a team is not worth the repeated efforts to deal with it.

CHAPTER

Resolving Team Disagreement

10

With the first whiffs of team conflict, it is easy to jump to the conclusion that there are trust issues on a team, but conflict is not - in and of itself - a bad thing for teams. In fact, without a little tension on the team now and again I suspect there will be a lack of innovation and legitimate/important change. Progress's path often runs through team conflict.

How should a manager deal with team conflict? I recommend conflict-management training for the group. It gives everyone a baseline of skills to manage conflict thoughtfully, and it provides a common lexicon or language for the team to use when dealing with conflict. In a sense, it makes conflict resolution more efficient.

I often use the "1-2-3 approach" to resolve team disagreements. Disagreements are those situations that have not yet elevated themselves

> Disagreements are those situations that have not yet elevated themselves to full-blown conflicts, but could elevate if they are not handled well.

to full-blown conflicts, but could elevate if they are not handled well. This technique heads off any serious conflicts by jumping on disagreements early and depersonalizing them.

When there is a legitimate disagreement on the team, I encourage each person to bring three things to the table:

1. the data they have to back up their point of view

2. any experiences that informs their point of view

3. any assumptions or beliefs that are informing their point of view

Once all the data, experiences, assumptions, and beliefs are on the table, the team can begin the collaborative debate process. If the team's alignment, process, and relationships are in a healthy place, this collaboration will resolve the disagreement most of the time. It is a classic two-heads-are-better-than-one moment. The manager simply needs to effectively facilitate the team collaboration.

Behind this 1-2-3 framework is something kind of profound. The manager is leveraging three things: group knowledge, group diversity, and group bias. It acknowledges that diversity of any kind—when managed well—can improve team performance and productivity. This approach also acknowledges that we all bring our biases to the table in the form of assumptions and beliefs. These assumptions and beliefs may linger in the background of team conversations. They need to be pulled forward and made explicit by the team to honestly resolve disagreements.

Managing this collaborative process when disagreements surface is partly about managing group dynamics.

Managing Group Dynamics

11

Group dynamics are the effective or ineffective interactions between team members in team settings—usually team meetings. While everyone on a team carries responsibility for productive behavior in team settings, the manager is accountable for ensuring team interactions are productive and respectful.

Managers typically get very little training in how to manage group dynamics. It is beyond the scope of this little book to do the topic justice, but it is important to wade into the shallow end of the pool and comment briefly on the role of a manager when tending to this important duty.

Two elements of emotional intelligence that are foundational skills for managing group dynamics are the ability to read the emotional tenor of a room and the ability to effectively respond to or guide those emotions to a productive place.

> When a manager can accurately read a room and direct (or redirect) their team's behaviors toward productive conversations and action, team success can follow more easily.

When a manager can accurately read a room and direct (or redirect) their team's behaviors toward productive conversations and action, team success can follow more easily.

The 1-2-3 approach to resolving team disagreement is a nice example of managing a team dynamic. When disagreements surface in a team setting, there is always the possibility that emotions will flair as positions are taken and defensiveness sets in. A savvy manager understands this danger and uses the 1-2-3 approach to head off any serious conflict. This approach can sometimes depersonalize disagreement.

Let's consider three common group dynamics situations:

- Who do people look at when they talk?
- Who talks the most? Who hardly says anything?
- Who is involved in group decisions?

Who do people look at when they talk? Not everyone is afforded the same level of attention in team meetings. In any given group, some people get the full attention of others when they speak, and others do not. Sometimes it is about power. Those with the power to decide or reward get full attention, and those without power receive less attention when they speak. Sometimes it is about seniority. Those with more experience get full attention, and those with little seniority get less. It can cut the other way as well. I have seen circumstances where the new folks get the attention while the old guard is ignored. Sometimes it is about competency. Those with more skills and knowledge get full attention, and those with less to offer get less attention. Sometimes it can be about gender. Research certainly supports the assertion that often when men speak, more attention is given to them than when women speak.

There are more reasons why some people receive more attention than others in group settings. This dynamic should be managed for two reasons: First, giving someone your attention when he or she speaks is a show of respect. Without respect, trust can be damaged. We know how important trust is to a team's success. Second, being too selective in who we give our attention to can increase the likelihood of sub-optimizing the team's productivity. Insights, good ideas, and diverse perspectives can come from any quarter on the team. Inattention could mean certain insights, ideas, and diverse perspectives are overlooked or lost.

What can a manager do to ensure attention is given to everyone who speaks? First, explicitly require that each member of the team gives his or her undivided attention to their colleagues. Make it a ground rule. Second, be the role model. Make sure your attention does not wander when certain people speak. Third, redirect if a team member focuses all their attention on you as the manager and not the speaker. A casual gesture with the hand or eyes can encourage the speaker to turn their attention to the group. Some managers say, "Share it with the group," which can redirect the conversation to the team.

Who talks the most? Who hardly says anything? There are several reasons why uneven airtime exists on teams. Some of those reasons are rooted in personal insecurity. Some people are intimidated by speaking in group settings. They feel they have little offer or worry they will say something stupid. The reverse can also be true. Some talkative folks are simply playing out their insecurities by talking a bunch and are worried they won't be heard.

It is unrealistic to expect a team of six people to speak for exactly ten minutes each in a one-hour team meeting. Extroverts may process their thoughts by speaking about them. Some introverts like to process their thoughts before speaking. Those are normal human dynamics.

What can a manager to do ensure that everyone who needs to weigh in gets to weigh in? What should be done about those insecurities? A manager should take note of the balance of extroverts and introverts on their teams. A Myers-Briggs Type Indicator can uncover extrovert/introvert tendencies, and sharing those tendencies can be quite helpful. The team will begin to understand why some speak more than others, and that tendency is normalized. Allow the extroverts to have the floor earlier—but be sure to invite the introverts into the discussion before it ends. To help give introverts a little extra time, send meeting agendas and pre-reads out ahead of meetings so they can process and be prepared.

For those who are insecure about their participation in team meetings, discuss it with them privately. Try to understand why they hesitate or chatter on. With that knowledge, build an action plan for more productive interactions. For the insecure introvert, ease them into the party by asking them to speak briefly on a subject they are confident about. If that goes well, have them repeat and see, over time, if they start contributing more. Ask them to go out on a limb and ask one question in each meeting. For the insecure extrovert, ask them to throttle back on their impromptu airtime and give them planned airtime on a subject they are confident about. If they tend to dominate the conversation by asking too many questions, ask them to limit their questions to one per team meeting for a while and see if that selective questioning makes them more productive.

Who is involved in group decisions? Here we return to two themes we've touched on earlier, decision rights and the value of collaboration when making decisions. When decision rights are understood by the team, decision making in group situations are easier. When it is unclear who owns the decision right team meetings can become, at one extreme, a tug-of-war between team members trying to own the decision and, at the other extreme, a conversation that goes nowhere since no one steps up to make the decision.

Should everyone on a team be involved in the decision? I think it depends on whether they have something of value to contribute to the decision. In the RACI model, the C represents *consulted* because the input of others, before a decision is made, helps ensure an issue or opportunity has been fully discussed and all points of view are considered. Research shows that including multiple points of view improves the quality of decisions when the collaborative process is managed well. So, as managers, if we are going to err, we should err on the inclusion of team input for decisions rather than the exclusion of that input.

The word *inclusion* should not be lost on you. Most organizations strive to create inclusive work environments. A manager can contribute to this goal by developing a collaborative decision-making process that taps the perspectives of the many while maintaining the effectiveness and efficiency of single, clear points of accountability.

Also, expanding the decision process to include the input of others provides opportunities to help people develop and grow as their participation in the process builds skills and confidence. Make sure the decision rights are clear and treat the rest of the team like consultants.

Managers may face dozens of group dynamics during their careers. Some of those situations require fancy managerial footwork since human behavior is complex, but many situations simply require paying attention to group dynamics and using the tools associated with the alignment, process, and relationship framework—naming decision rights, the 1-2-3 approach to disagreement, or leveraging collaboration—to guide the team to a better place.

How can you improve at managing team dynamics? Take note of dynamics in team meetings and devise plans for addressing any unproductive trends. Talk with other managers about how they manage team dynamics. Read articles about the topic. Raising your team dynamics acumen will make you a better manager.

The Influence of Team Culture

12

This book is about successfully managing teams. Good alignment, process, and relationships are the necessary conditions for that success, but there is a wild card that needs to be taken into consideration: team culture.

In programs, I refer to team culture as the seas upon which the three boats of alignment, process, and relationship must sail. A calm cultural sea means smooth sailing. Turbulent cultural seas make the job a little harder.

Culture is always a tricky topic. The definition can be elusive, and changing a culture seems daunting, but teams are smaller than organizations, and with some effort and the right tools, managers can successfully shape the culture and let the alignment, process, and relationship efforts pay dividends.

There are several tools to help managers with their team culture efforts. My favorite is an assessment tool called the Group Styles Inventory™ (GSI), which was developed by Human Synergistics. This tool is part of a suite of diagnostic surveys focused on individual, team, and organizational performance. The GSI is specifically designed to generate insights about teams and measures twelve team styles.[1] A style is a description of how a team plays

---

[1] Style names are from the *Group Styles Inventory*™ (GSI). Research and development by Robert A. Cooke, PhD, and J. Clayton Lafferty, PhD. Copyright © 1990–2018 by Human Synergistics International. All rights reserved. Used by permission.

out its culture and how members experience the team. Four of the styles are *constructive*, and they are characteristic of effective or high-performing teams. The other eight styles are defensive (passive-defensive and aggressive-defensive), and they are consistent with less effective teams.

Constructive Styles

- The achievement style speaks to how effective the team is at setting and achieving goals. Effective teams consistently display this style.
- The self-actualizing style speaks to how enthusiastic and energized the team is about its work. Effective teams consistently display this style.
- The humanistic-encouraging style speaks to how team members successfully develop and motivate one another. Effective teams consistently display this style.
- The affiliative style speaks to the quality of the team's cooperation and interpersonal relationships. Effective teams consistently display this style.

Passive and Aggressive (Defensive) Styles

- The approval style reflects a team's tendency toward excessive tactfulness and acceptance that inhibits direct communications.
- The conventional style reflects a team's tendency to resist or set aside new ideas and maintain the status quo.
- The dependent style reflects team members' tendency to ask for assistance and depend on each other to make decisions for them.
- The avoidance style reflects the team's tendency to be evasive when decisiveness is needed and play it safe to minimize risks.
- The oppositional style reflects the team's tendency to criticize, challenge, and oppose ideas without proper consideration.

- The power style reflects the team's tendency to force issues (rather than discuss and consider them) and refuse to compromise.
- The competitive style reflects the team's preference for winning points rather than solving problems.
- The perfectionistic style reflects the team's tendency to get hung up on details.

This summary does not do justice to the depth and power of this tool and its insights.[2] I highly recommend getting this assessment and using it with your team. However, this summary illustrates the challenges of working on alignment, process, and relationships, and it directs us to potential solutions for those challenges.

Imagine a team has a very low score on the achievement style and high scores on the dependent and avoidance styles. Efforts to align the team around specific goals and efforts to clarify specific roles so processes can go smoothly will likely be met with resistance. Plans will come together slowly. Alternative plans will rarely be considered. Members might fail to take on their share of responsibilities and be reluctant to commit to solutions. The manager will need to adjust expectations of behaviors that are more consistent with the achievement style and less consistent with the dependent and avoidance styles. Training on how to set goals might be needed. Peer pressure might need to be applied to get folks to follow the lead of better performers.

Another challenging team style profile might be low humanistic-encouraging and affiliative styles and a high oppositional style. In this circumstance, the team dynamic would be highlighted by disagreement without resolution, lots of defending of people's points of view, people not helping one another, and conversations marked by tension. Efforts to improve relationships will probably not be wildly successful in that environment. The

---

[2] For more information about the GSI, visit www.humansynergistics.com. A detailed explanation of the circumplex and the twelve styles can be found at www.humansynergistics.com/about-us/the-circumplex.

manager will need to adjust expectations of behaviors. Peer coaching might be embedded in each team member's performance goals. Clear, people-oriented ground rules about how meetings are run and attended might be necessary.

In both examples, behavior adjustment is key. Culture is all about behavioral norms and changing a team's culture ultimately is going to be about changing behaviors. Changing behaviors is not always easy, but managers facing defensive styles need to take actions to reap real benefits from their alignment, process, and relationship efforts.

It's beyond the scope of this book to get into the nitty-gritty of changing behaviors, but consider one important rule of thumb: address the will and skill needed to change a behavior. Managers need to pay attention to the willingness of team members to change their behaviors and the skills required to make those changes.

There are several ways to address the will to change behaviors. Sell the benefits by explaining what's in it for them and the team can help. Peer pressure may also work. Certain reward-and-consequence systems can influence someone's will to change. Make the right behaviors part of team members' performance goals and reward them for displaying those behaviors. On the skills side, train and give feedback on new behaviors via coaching or mentoring. Certain skills can be enhanced with the use of new tools or better information.

Pay attention to your team's culture. Go out and invest in a tool like the GSI and attend to the results thoughtfully.

When One Person Makes It Hard on the Whole Team

13

Sometimes a team is doing fine. Alignment, process, and relationships are good, and productivity may be perfectly acceptable—or even stellar—but one person on the team is causing heartburn. Their behavior is counterproductive and is probably sub-optimizing the performance of the other team members. Worse, their presence may be a prelude to other team issues if not addressed properly. This is a team issue in the form of an individual performance problem.

An adept use of the alignment, process, relationships framework can help managers deal with this performance problem. The following four scenarios will explore this issue. Consider three questions as you read each scenario:

· What team issues are you most worried about in each scenario?
· Would you regard this issue as more of an alignment, a process, or a relationship issue?
· What would you do in each of these situations?

***

Rick, a recent college graduate, has been a member of your team for about one year. He is a customer service representative in your call center. While he started off kind of slow in his role, everything seemed to click after a few months. He has done a fine job ever since. He is a solid performer and is good with customers on the phone.

Each member of your team has been assigned to a new client implementation team in addition to their duties on the phone. Rick's team meets once a week to discuss progress and next steps toward implementation.

The team has been struggling to get their agreed-upon tasks done and move the project forward. There has been some tension in meetings that you want to address. You raise this issue with the team, and the first two team members mention Rick not completing some internal manager interviews as the reason they could not get their work done. Rick indicates he struggled to get the interviews scheduled with the managers.

When a frustrated member of the team encouraged Rick to get the interviews scheduled and get on with it, Rick lost his temper. He said he was having problems scheduling the interviews—not that he hadn't scheduled them. He pointed out that others around the table had not completed their to-do lists and wondered why he was being singled out.

Some words were exchanged between Rick and another team member before things calmed down. Everyone finally agreed to a time line for completing their tasks, but Rick was clearly shaken as he left the meeting.

***

When I share this scenario in training programs, participants generally worry about the engagement of Rick and the freedom to blame in the meeting. Using GSI terms, some oppositional or competitive style seems to be surfacing.

Relationships are fraying, and most groups see the underlying issue as alignment or process. Perhaps Rick is working toward a different set of goals. There may be a lack of clarity about each team member's responsibilities, particularly with deliverables.

The recommendation is often to have the manager revisit goals and responsibilities with the whole group and have separate conversations with

Rick to check in with his engagement and the frustrated team member to clarify acceptable team behaviors (avoiding the blame game).

Some groups question Rick's statement about being singled out. If Rick was the only young person in the room, was there some type of generational bias on display? Some groups conclude this needs to be on the manager's radar.

***

Bree joined the field-service team as a traveling technician about thirty days ago. She came from a competitor. Overall, she has about fifteen years of relevant experience, including a short time as a driver for a municipality. Her specialty as a technical expert is with electronic systems, and she has a knack for pointing out where the problem is when electronics seems to be the issue. Bree enjoys discussions in this technical area.

As soon as Bree joined the team, she immediately began making changes to the standard routines in the mobile service area. She adjusted schedules with little warning, shifted technicians around the various duty stations before understanding their skills, and put two employees on warning without consulting her manager or HR, or documenting what the issues were. Complaints have been steadily rising from team members, and you are concerned the situation is going to get out of hand.

***

When I have shared this scenario, groups are concerned about Bree's impact on the team and the customers. There is an urgency to deal with Bree. It is not time to sit back and let it play out.

There is general agreement that the root cause here is process—and a complete lack of clarity about roles, responsibilities, and appropriate use of standard processes.

The manager must sit down with Bree and recalibrate everything. If she continues her behavior, there is a trust issue at play. Most groups suggest dismissal, but the manager should explore the process side of the issue before that action is considered.

***

Debra is a sweet soul who joined the organization many years ago and asked to join your team about four months before you became manager.

Everyone on the team likes Debra, but they all have the same issue: she cannot seem to get her work done quickly enough to complete the client work on time. Your team's process requires great coordination between members, each attending to an important piece of the final product.

Complaints about Debra have been delayed because of her likability, but other team members have been picking up part of her workload to help her out and get the job done.

You provided Debra with additional training and even coaching, but it hasn't helped the situation. The team's productivity is being dragged down by Debra, and your boss has asked you to deal with it once and for all—one way or another.

***

When I share this scenario, they point out how Debra's team is like a football team. Weak effort by one affects the whole team. That is the problem. Most seem to have had a Debra in their lives, and there is sympathy along with the worry.

The root issue is relationship—specifically professional trust. Since efforts to remedy the issue have failed, the conclusion of most people is that Debra must go. The hope is always that there is a niche for her someplace else in the organization where her talents can match the required effort.

***

Nate is a star performer and has been one for a while. Within a year of joining the team, his stellar performance exceeded everyone else. Everyone is aware that his work is the best, but he keeps a reasonably low profile. Modest might be a good way to describe his nature.

In a recent stretch, client demands on the team suddenly increased, which caused the need for everyone except for Nate to work harder and even more hours. Nate can work a normal workweek and still get everything on his plate done. While everyone else was working until seven, Nate was strolling out the door at five with his work done and done well.

One evening, as the team is finishing up around seven thirty, you hear them complaining about Nate: "He is not a team player. If he cared about the team, he would stay and help out the rest of us."

***

Most participants see this scenario as the opposite of Debra's situation. First, there is an inference that this team is more like a wrestling team where work is individualized. Second, Nate is a very good performer. And finally, while not unlikeable, Nate is perhaps unapproachable.

Groups usually see this as a process issue since expectations for team members have not been appropriately set. The manager needs to set the expectation that Nate should hang around and help others until the work is done or explain to the team that the work is individualized and everyone can go when their work is done.

Regardless of which approach is taken, most agree that Nate's expertise should be tapped. At a minimum, Nate should be sharing his best practices with the team and perhaps even coaching others.

Consider such scenarios in your workplace when an individual is creating issues for your team. When you examine the scenario, is the root cause an alignment issue, a process issue, or a relationship issue? Don't be fooled. Many times, what presents itself as a relationship issue (Nate is leaving early, and we don't like it) is an alignment or process issue. Look for the root cause if you can. The casual pecking order to this alignment, process, and relationship framework holds true for addressing individual performance issues with team implications. Use the framework as a checklist to make sure you address the real causes of bad behavior in the workplace—and not just the symptoms.

Some Final Thoughts

14

Supreme Court Justice Oliver Wendell Holmes reportedly said, "I wouldn't give a fig for the simplicity on the near side

> "I wouldn't give a fig for the simplicity on the near side of complexity, but I would give my right arm for the simplicity on the far side of complexity."

of complexity, but I would give my right arm for the simplicity on the far side of complexity."

I wrote this book with this thought in mind. I know management is a complex endeavor. My hope is the simplicity of the alignment, process, and relationship framework proves a useful blueprint for sorting out that complexity. It is not intended to address every team issue we face as managers, but it has proven to be a useful mental model for addressing many team issues.

Now that you are about to close this book, what next? Here is the basic blueprint:

First, use the alignment, process, and relationship questions as a guide for improving your management expertise. I have included those questions in the appendix.

Second, address any alignment issues first. Remember, there is casual pecking order to this framework: align, process, relationships. Make sure the team's goals are clear and aligned with your organization's goals and your customer's needs.

Third, address any blatant process issues. Make sure the team roles, decision rights, and work processes are understood. Give them the feedback they need to execute on those processes.

Fourth, address relationship issues. Seek to build trust, develop emotional intelligence, and tend to and be vigilant about those group dynamics. If someone on the team is disrupting the team with their behavior, address it quickly and thoughtfully. Don't let it linger. Use the alignment, process, relationship framework as a diagnostic tool.

Fifth, consider using a tool like GSI to name and then address your team's culture.

Finally, seek out good management role models in your workplace and talk with them about how they manage their teams. Kick around best practices, steal their best ideas, and try them out.

Good luck with all your managerial efforts. Strive for progress—not perfection.

Appendix

Alignment is about team goals:

- Are your team goals explicit and clear?
- Are the metrics for these goals explicit and clear?
- Does your team have key behavioral goals the whole team understands and conforms to? Can you link those behavioral goals to other, more business-oriented goals?
- Do your team goals align with your department and organizational goals?
- Do you incent your team to achieve the stated goals?

Process is about team execution:

- Are members of your team clear about their roles and responsibilities? Are the decision rights of your team members clear to each of them?
- Is there a clear purpose for your team meetings? Are there standing agenda items for these meetings?
- Is there an opportunity for your team to assess its performance in a team setting? Does this opportunity to assess lead to improvements in team alignment, process, and relationships?
- Are your team's work processes understood and aligned with larger, organizational goals?

Relationships are about team dynamics:

- Does your team trust each other professionally and personally?
- Are legitimate disagreements on your team handled effectively?

- Does each member of your team have a reasonable amount of emotional intelligence?
- Are the group dynamics when the group is together healthy and productive?

Recommended Reading

Much of what I have presented in this book has come from my experiences and those of hundreds of others who have shaped my thinking on management. There have been some books that have also shaped my thinking, and I would recommend each of them for anyone interested in digging deeper into management and team management.

Early in this book, I mentioned two classic works on team management. I recommend you read them both.

- Peter Lencioni. *The Five Dysfunctions of a Team*. Jossey-Bass, 2002.
- Jon Katzenback and Douglas Smith. *The Wisdom of Teams*. Harvard Business School Press, 1993.

Here is a more contemporary book focuses on how teams connect and successfully interact with other teams.

- Chris Fussell with C. W. Goodyear. *One Mission*. Portfolio Penguin, 2017.

For some fun (and if you are a basketball fan), Phil Jackson's *Eleven Rings* explains how someone can build a successful team around one person on a team who is clearly a superior performer and still instill a team-oriented culture.

- Phil Jackson and Hugh Delehanty. *Eleven Rings*. Penguin Books, 2014.

If you enjoyed the chapter on team culture, you might enjoy Peter Fuda's book on leadership, which uses the same Human Synergistics framework applied to building leadership skills.

- Peter Fuda. *Leadership Transformation*. Houghton Mifflin Harcourt, 2013.

Simple Rules explores the value simple frameworks give to managers as they go about their daily work. If you are interested the effective use of simple rules in the workplace, this might be a good book to read. My continued work with managers and leaders has been influenced by this book.

- Donald Sull and Kathleen Eisenhardt. *Simple Rules.* Mariner, 2015.

Wiser: Getting Beyond Groupthink to Make Groups Smarter is one of the best books I've read on wisely managing group dynamics. It challenges a lot of conventional wisdom yet still delivers some practical advice.

- Cass Sunstein and Reid Hastie. *Wiser: Getting Beyond Groupthink to Make Groups Smarter.* Harvard Business Review Press. 2015.

I never miss an opportunity to recommend one of my favorite books about management and the job of a manager:

- Linda Hill and Kent Lineback. *Being the Boss.* Boston: Harvard Business Review, 2011.

About the Author

Steve King is the retired executive director for the Center for Professional and Executive Development at the University of Wisconsin's School of Business and the president of the SDK Group, which specializes in helping organizations find solutions for their business-related talent management issues.

Steve teaches at the University of Wisconsin–Madison and Northwestern University.

Steve spent more than twenty-five years leading in corporate settings. He was the senior vice president of human resources for Hewitt Associates, a global HR consulting and outsourcing firm. He also served as the VP of global talent management for Baxter Healthcare, faculty leader for the Bank of Montreal's Institute for Learning in Toronto, and vice president of management and professional development for Harris Bank in Chicago.

Steve lives in Madison, Wisconsin, and is the author of two other books on management: *Brag, Worry, Wonder, Bet* and *Six Conversations*.